ANIMAL SAFARI

Gorillas

by Derek Zobel

BELLWETHER MEDIA • MINNEAPOLIS, MN

BLASTOFF! READERS

Note to Librarians, Teachers, and Parents:

Blastoff! Readers are carefully developed by literacy experts and combine standards-based content with developmentally appropriate text.

Level 1 provides the most support through repetition of high-frequency words, light text, predictable sentence patterns, and strong visual support.

Level 2 offers early readers a bit more challenge through varied simple sentences, increased text load, and less repetition of high-frequency words.

Level 3 advances early-fluent readers toward fluency through increased text and concept load, less reliance on visuals, longer sentences, and more literary language.

Level 4 builds reading stamina by providing more text per page, increased use of punctuation, greater variation in sentence patterns, and increasingly challenging vocabulary.

Level 5 encourages children to move from "learning to read" to "reading to learn" by providing even more text, varied writing styles, and less familiar topics.

Whichever book is right for your reader, Blastoff! Readers are the perfect books to build confidence and encourage a love of reading that will last a lifetime!

This edition first published in 2012 by Bellwether Media, Inc.

No part of this publication may be reproduced in whole or in part without written permission of the publisher. For information regarding permission, write to Bellwether Media, Inc., Attention: Permissions Department, 5357 Penn Avenue South, Minneapolis, MN 55419.

Library of Congress Cataloging-in-Publication Data
Zobel, Derek, 1983-
Gorillas / by Derek Zobel.
    p. cm. – (Blastoff! Readers. Animal safari)
Includes bibliographical references and index.
Summary: "Developed by literacy experts for students in kindergarten through grade three, this book introduces gorillas to young readers through leveled text and related photos"–Provided by publisher.
ISBN 978-1-60014-605-3 (hardcover : alk. paper)
1. Gorilla–Juvenile literature. I. Title.
QL737.P96Z63 2011
599.884–dc22   2011006240

Printed in the United States of America, North Mankato, MN.

080111   1187

Contents

What Are Gorillas?

Gorillas are the largest **primates** on Earth.

They live in forests and on mountains. They build nests in trees and in tall grass.

What Gorillas Eat

Gorillas eat many kinds of plants. They also eat **insects** and worms.

Troops

A group of gorillas is called a **troop**. A troop can have 5 to 30 gorillas.

Older males
have silver hair
on their backs.
The strongest male
is the troop leader.

The leader decides where the troop eats, sleeps, and moves. He also protects the troop.

Baby Gorillas

A female gorilla has one baby every three or four years.

The baby rides around on its mother's back.

It sleeps with its
mother at night.
Snuggle up gorillas!

Glossary

insects—small animals with six legs and hard outer bodies; insect bodies are divided into three parts.

primates—animals that use their hands to grasp food and other objects; primates are related to humans.

troop—a group of gorillas that lives together; the largest, strongest male in a troop is its leader.

To Learn More

AT THE LIBRARY

Nichols, Michael, and Elizabeth Carney.
Face to Face With Gorillas. Washington, D.C.:
National Geographic, 2009.

Simon, Seymour. *Gorillas.* New York, N.Y.:
HarperCollins Publishers, 2000.

Thomson, Sarah L. *Amazing Gorillas.* New
York, N.Y.: HarperCollins, 2005.

ON THE WEB

Learning more about
gorillas is as easy as 1, 2, 3.

1. Go to www.factsurfer.com.

2. Enter "gorillas" into
   the search box.

3. Click the "Surf" button and you will see a
   list of related Web sites.

With factsurfer.com, finding more information
is just a click away.

Index

The images in this book are reproduced through the courtesy of: Mike Price, front cover; Elliot Hurwitt, p. 5; Anup Shah / naturepl.com, p. 7 (top); Henry Wilson, p. 7 (left & right); Suzi Eszterhas / Minden Pictures, p. 9 (top); Doug Lemke, p. 9 (left); D. Kucharski & K. Kucharski, p. 9 (right); Thomas Marent / Minden Pictures, pp. 11, 13; Minden Pictures / Masterfile, p. 15; Suzi Eszterhas / Minden Pictures, p. 17; Juniors Bildarchiv / Alamy, p. 19; Getty Images, p. 21.

$22.76
5-12

T 567605